## PRAISE FOR MASHA MALKA AND
# The One Minute Coach

Of all the hundreds of self-development books I've read, there are only a handful that have moved me in the way Masha's words do. If you, too, are looking for information, perhaps that spark of inspiration, or ideas for implementation to take your life to the next level—then look no further. Masha's hard-won experiences and words of truth will be the catalyst to help you be the very best you can be.

**—Peter Thomson**
*leading UK strategist on business and personal growth*

Masha Malka is living proof of what can happen if human potential is allowed to express itself. This is a book that you can either read from cover to cover, or better yet, dip into whenever you have a few moments, so it is one for the briefcase as well as the bedside table. Highly recommended.

**—Richard G. Petty, MD,**
*author of Healing, Meaning and Purpose*

This is a simple, straightforward, yet powerful book. It is so readable, the action steps are not overwhelming—and, for those who follow it from beginning to end, it will have a profound effect.

**—Cheryl Alexander**
*executive coach and founder of Cheryl Alexander & Associates, USA*

I started reading the book, and I couldn't stop reading every word is like a gem! I love it!

**—Chani Goldstein**
*rabbi's wife, Jerusalem, Israel*

The One Minute Coach happened to be the first book since a long time that I finished reading, as lately I had a bad habit of starting many books and never finishing them. The structure of the book is so "reader friendly" and I could read any chapter at any time without loosing the plot. I loved it and I read some of the chapters a few times!!!!

**—Anna Zegzula**
*Co-Owner of KOMANDOR*
*Poland*

With the use of parables and stories and clever illustrations at the end of each section, the wisdom you get out of reading this book simply sticks. And the best part is that you'll feel really good in the process!

**—Luis David Llense**
*artist, Miami, USA*

In a world where many are scared to ask and listen to their inner voice, Masha gives us permission to take the time to do just that, on our terms and timetable.

**—Shari Haman**
*registered nurse and mother of two, Minneapolis, USA*

This is a truly inspirational book, very easy to read. It will improve your life and your thinking.

**—Ian Medina**
*international consultant in emerging economies, Miami, USA*

This transformational book is a minute-by-minute true guide and incredible motivator that any person, anywhere in the world, can take an action towards improvement."

**—Rick Yarosh**
*entrepreneur, Aventura, USA*

Love the book! The format is very effective—short, sweet ... and it just gets you thinking versus lots of heavy stuff ...

**—Leslie Moore**
*CEO of EquiUnity, Ebenezer, Australia*

*The One Minute Coach* delivers a powerful confidence boost and inspires us to change our lives one minute at a time. The format is uncomplicated, as are the fundamental principles we need to follow before we can lead.

**—Cindy Barnes**
*event organizer and founder of the Grapevine Club, Marbella, Spain*

It is like a whole little library rolled into one ... the perfect reference book for a better way of life.

**—Geraldine Daly**
*sales manager for Connectivity Warehouse, Malaga, Spain*

# The One Minute Coach™

Change Your Life
One Minute at a Time!

## Masha Malka

New York

# The One Minute Coach

Change Your Life One Minute at a Time!

## by Masha Malka

ISBN: 978-1-60037-468-5

Library of Congress Control Number: 2008929706

**Published by:**

MORGAN · JAMES
THE ENTREPRENEURIAL PUBLISHER ™
www.morganjamespublishing.com

Morgan James Publishing, LLC

1225 Franklin Ave. Ste 325

Garden City, NY 11530-1693

Toll Free 800-485-4943

www.MorganJamesPublishing.com

Habitat
for Humanity®
Peninsula
Building Partner

Artwork by **Anna Polonsky**
Editing by **Cary Johnston** caryjohnston@hotmail.com
Production design by **Gregory Korvin** gregk@telefonica.net
Cover photo and family photo by **Gary Edwards** www.edwardsx.com

*TO DORON,*
*For helping me become the person I am today and for your*
*unconditional support, love, strength, and wisdom...*

# CONTENTS

# FOREWORD by Cary Johnston

*(freelance journalist and former London-based BBC reporter)*

Some people are born into money. Some people are born into power. Most of us, however, just seem content to shrug our shoulders and settle for what little we appear to have, however unhappy that might make us feel. But is that really good enough? Masha Malka doesn't think so.

She greets you with an air of quiet confidence and, for someone so used to public speaking and dealing with the leaders of industry, it is a surprise to discover that Masha has a rather gentle voice and a disarming smile. Clearly, her power comes not from posturing, but from the knowledge that her tuition and methods have been proven to work. Only the occasional break in her accent gives a hint of her Eastern European roots.

The young Masha grew up in the Cold War atmosphere of a Soviet-controlled Ukraine, in a city called Kharkov, on the border with Russia. She may have had high ambitions for herself, but in the former Soviet Union, free and easy movement was hard to come by.

Not that the young Masha was desperate to leave. After all, the Soviet Union provided free education, free extracurricular activities, and free summer camps! For a youngster, this was like heaven. But her parents, themselves modestly employed, could foresee the future workplace limitations, and while Masha left school at the age of 15 and went to a dance college for two years, her mother toiled with the necessary bureaucracy to allow her to take her daughter out of the country—she'd been asking the authorities for nine years. A Jewish family, their initial aim was to head for Israel.

Finally, in the late eighties atmosphere of Mikhail Gorbachev's *perestroika* era, permission was granted, and Masha's parents were allowed to leave the Ukraine, taking their seventeen-year-old daughter, thirteen-year-old son, and sick grandfather with them. The problem was, when you left the Soviet Union, you left with nothing.

The authorities stripped them of their citizenship and, until their departure, Masha's mother wouldn't even let her play outside, for fear of reprisals from neighbours—such was the shame associated with abandoning the Soviet system. You were deemed to be an enemy of the state.

At the border, they were only allowed to take the equivalent of one hundred dollars each and were even denied a last group photo – no mementos, no chance of return, and no one in the family was able to speak anything other than Russian. They were now refugees and, for Masha, this was to be the beginning of the dark time …

The family was first sent to Vienna, a normal procedure at the time. There, they would be processed and told which Western country might accept them. For three months, they were in limbo, but even in Vienna, the culture shock was immense. Masha's mother once sent her to a supermarket to buy some jam. A bewildered Masha surveyed the twenty different jams on the shelf and experienced her first dose of cultural paralysis, spending the next two hours examining the different labels. After all, why didn't they make things easy and just produce one kind?

One day, on a visit to a public swimming pool, Masha saw a woman bathing topless and ran up to her to inform the poor lady that maybe she had lost her clothes and could she help her find them?

Eventually, the United States was chosen as their next destination, but adjusting to a new lifestyle was difficult, especially without a firm grasp of the English language. Her parents could only get cleaning jobs, so money was tight, and the young Masha was sent to an American high school. The shock of liberal dress codes and complete freedom of speech was out of this world. For her, it was like another planet!

But, nonetheless, she persevered in her studies and, although at first she found the English language difficult to master, she was exceptional at mathematics – a universal language all its own. Different part-time jobs followed to help make ends meet. Salesperson, cashier, and assistant at the University of Miami, which, at the time housed one of only two public scanners in the whole of the United States. For her, it felt like the greatest privilege and achievement to be in charge of using it!

But she had no idea what to do with her life, and, while America seemed like the land of plenty, it can also be a lonely place for one raised in a totally different system. It seemed, especially in the go-getting atmosphere of the United States, that all the people around her knew exactly what they wanted and where they were going. Culturally lost and professionally unsure, Masha had turned from being a confident, outgoing individual to an introverted and depressed young lady, with little or no self-esteem.

It's here that the turning point came, when, by chance, she came across a life-coaching tape made by Brian Tracy (see References and Recommended Reading list) and discovered that self-esteem and the ability to be responsible for your own life were the secrets to great success. By taking those seeds and with years of painstaking research, Masha not only learned to grow a new life for herself, but is now willing and able to share her discoveries with *you*, in the pages of this book.

It's not about forcing change; it's about being a catalyst for change. You can only help people who want to be helped, and Masha became an expert in guiding people to answer the questions they already knew the answers to, but were unwilling or unable to face. It's about encouragement. It's about striving to be where you want to be. It's about enjoying your life to the fullest.

Today, Masha's confidence (and smile!) comes from living the life she wants to live in southern Spain. Married with three children, she is still more than able to pursue her career on her terms. Her journey from hardship to happiness is proof that anyone is capable of positive change. So open your mind, and let Masha show you how to make the most of your talents. Your new life starts here ...

# INTRODUCTION

Dear friend,

Where will you be one year from now?

Will you be doing the same things, going to the same places, spending time with the same people, wishing the same things, and realizing that with each year that passes, those wishes will probably never materialize?

Or will you be moving rapidly towards the life of your dreams, having made the necessary changes in your mentality, having taken necessary action steps, and feeling great about your future, your progress, and yourself as a person?

The choice is *yours!*

By buying this book, you have already made a choice that puts you in a group of people who care about their future, their growth, and their overall happiness and fulfilment in life. Although I wish I could talk to you face-to-face, I am honored to speak to you through the words on these pages, and I am grateful to you for helping me fulfil my purpose in life!

I have designed the book using *Accelerated Learning* techniques and neuro-linguistic programming to make it easy for you to read and assimilate the information and, more importantly, to apply it in your day-to-day life. There are fifty-two inspirational messages plus introduction and conclusion, with an application/action step for each message. You can read and apply one a week for the duration of the year, or you can use the book as a reference guide and consult it on specific topics as needed.

*How* you use the book is not as important as *what* you do with the information in it. To make a real difference in your life requires not just an understanding of what would make it different but also consistent, focused action.

Without taking up any more of your valuable time, let me thank you for buying *The One Minute Coach* and welcome you on an exciting journey of self-discovery and growth!

Your partner in success,

PART 1

FREEDOM TO BE WHO YOU ARE

# Whose Life Are You Living?

*Everything great was created starting with a decision – your new life is no exception.*

—**Masha Malka**

Have you ever felt like you are living someone else's life? It is one of the worst feelings one can experience, and most of us, at some point, do feel this way!

The first and most important step to living a fulfilling and authentic life that is totally and wonderfully *yours* is to realize that it's *your* life, and you deserve to live it on *your* terms. The next step is to remember what life you are meant to live, to go back to *who you really are*, and to let your passions and true personal desires surface again.

The process is more difficult for some than others, but the benefits are well worth it! The following are some of the benefits of living *your* life:

- Life has meaning and purpose.
- Your self-esteem shoots up.
- You deal with life's obstacles effectively.
- People just want to be with you.
- You attract positivity to your life.
- You feel fulfilled and happy.

The benefits are many and cannot all be described in words, but the main reason for living *your* life is this: *you deserve to*!

I, myself, have been in the darkness of not knowing *who am I* and *what am I meant to do*, as well as not experiencing the fulfilment of living a life of purpose. I have made the journey, and I have seen others do it. Now, it is *your* turn. I believe that every one of us deserves to live an authentic life – a fulfilling and happy life. I have made it my purpose to help as many people as I can to achieve that.

# Action Steps

1. Start a journal to follow your progress as you go through this book.
2. Decide on the time of the day that you will spend focusing on yourself – reading, writing, reflecting, applying what you learn – and anything else that helps you grow and move in the direction you want to go.

# The "Impossible" Is Often the Untried

*What is now proved was once impossible.*
> —**William Blake** (1757–1827, British poet and artist)

*If you deliberately plan on being less than you are capable of being, then I warn you that you'll be unhappy for the rest of your life.*
> —**Abraham H. Maslow** (1908–1970, American psychologist)

Do you believe it is possible for you to become fulfilled and successful in all areas of your life?

You might know an unforgettable example of making the impossible possible, achieved by Roger Bannister on May 6, 1954. For centuries before that date, it was considered humanly impossible to run a mile in under four minutes. There was a widespread belief that, if you did, your heart would explode!

Roger Bannister believed something different and proved to the world that what was considered to be impossible was not so. The amazing fact is not just that Mr. Bannister was able to run a mile in less than four minutes, but that just one year later, thirty-seven other people around the world followed his example, and, within two years, three hundred runners managed to break the previously "impossible" record!

Why?

Because whatever you believe, becomes your self-fulfilling prophecy. If you believe it is impossible for you to become successful and fulfilled in all areas of your life, then it is very unlikely that you will. However, if you see someone in the same position as you, who has "made it," and you change your belief system because of that example, then you will open the door to the great possibility of becoming and getting all that you want in life.

# Action Steps

1. Remind yourself daily that, if you desire something with all your heart and soul, it is because you are meant to have it. One of the wisest persons who ever lived, Rebbe Nachman of Breslov (1772–1810), points out: "Always remember, you are never given an obstacle you cannot overcome."

2. Create an unshakable belief in your ability to reach your goals. When you follow your dreams and believe you can reach them, everything in life supports you. Even the obstacles you come across along the way are there to teach you and ultimately help you get to where you want to be.

# If They Can Do It, So Can You!

*One must have the adventurous daring to accept oneself as a bundle of possibilities and undertake the most interesting game in the world—making the most of one's best.*
> —**Harry Emerson Fosdick** (1878–1969, American Baptist pastor)

*To be fully alive is to feel that everything is possible.*
> —**Eric Hoffer** (1902–1983, American writer)

Are you making the most of your best?

When Pete Sampras' schoolmates were out playing and socializing, Pete practiced his tennis. Years later, when Pete was already the top tennis player in the world, he did things differently again. He took his whole game apart in order to raise himself to a new level. It paid off. He went on to beat the then record of twelve Grand Slam Singles titles.

When everyone around Bill Gates was skeptical about the widespread usage of computers, Bill envisaged a PC in every home. He took appropriate actions based on his vision, and the rest is history.

Celine Dion dreamt of being an internationally acclaimed singer from the age of five.

Jim Carrey wrote himself a cheque for $20 million when he was a factory floor cleaner and carried it around with him in his wallet. In 1995, he was offered that same amount for his role in the movie *The Cable Guy*!

What is it that these people have in common that enabled them to do what they did?
What enabled them to stand out from the crowd?
How can you do the same?

# Action Steps

1. The first and most important thing you have to do is *believe* that what you want to achieve is possible!
2. Learn as much as you can in that area, and take consistent focused action until you achieve it.

# Are You Starving Your Soul?

*The level of success and fulfilment you enjoy in your life is the result of how well you contribute to your purpose.*

—**Masha Malka**

What is your purpose in life? Is it important to stop and think about it?

I believe it is. Because having a clear purpose in life—making a difference in the lives of others—happens to be one of the greatest human hungers! If you don't have a clear purpose, then you are starving your soul!

According to Robin Sharma, author of the best-selling book *The Monk Who Sold His Ferrari*, "People have a deep inner need to be a part of something larger than themselves." Whether we are speaking of the CEO or the factory floor cleaner, every human being needs to feel that he or she is making some sort of contribution.

Richard J. Leider has made it his purpose to help others discover theirs. In his book *The Power of Purpose*, he states: "Purpose is the conscious choice of what, where, and how to make a positive contribution to our world. It is the theme, quality, or passion we choose to center our lives around."

Rediscovering what makes you tick – what you are passionate about – is essential to living the life you desire and deserve! If what you do on a daily basis is not aligned with your talents, passion, and purpose in life, then you will not be very eager to get up in the morning.

*If your life is worth living, it is worth living with purpose!*

—**Masha Malka**

# Action Steps

If you don't have a compelling reason to get up in the morning — a purpose that drives you to do what you do — then make it your primary goal to find out what it is. Here are some steps that will help you with your discovery:

1. Pay attention to what you are passionate about - passion and purpose go hand in hand.
2. Imagine yourself being very old and analyzing your life. What achievements are you most proud of?
3. Finally, ask yourself this powerful question: "If I had all the money and time I needed and could do anything, knowing without a doubt that I would succeed, what would I do?"

Enjoy the process, and remember that it is never too early or too late to start living a life of purpose. Most likely, you have been doing it for years without even realizing it!

# What Fulfills You?

*People who live happy and fulfilling lives are those who know what they want and do not settle for anything less than that!*

**—Masha Malka**

What fulfilment means to you is intensely personal. When people first think about it, they might focus on outward measures of success, such as a great job, enough money, or a certain lifestyle. But if you focus deeper, you will realize that true fulfilment is not about having more. It is not about what fills your pockets or closets; it is about what fills your heart and your soul.

A fulfilling life is a valued life. What are your top values? Are they being honored?

Sorting out your values is a way of sorting out life choices, because when the choices honor your values, life is more satisfying and seems almost effortless.

Also, although achieving a certain goal can be very fulfilling, you often find that this kind of fulfilment is not the finish line. At its deepest level, fulfilment is about finding and experiencing a life of purpose; it is about living by your values.

It is about reaching your full potential.

# Action Steps

1. Most people live their lives caught up in a daily routine, never stopping and asking themselves "What is my purpose? What are my core values? What really fulfills me?" If you have never thought about purpose and values before, then the first step is to do just that. Spend time with yourself, thinking about your life. Think about where you are going and what makes you really happy.

2. Realize that there is no right or wrong purpose or right or wrong set of values; there is only *your* purpose and *your* set of values – the ones that feel right to your heart!

# The Gift of Personal Freedom

*Don't say "If I could, I would." Say instead "If I can, I will."*

—**Jim Rohn** (motivational coach)

In preschool, the children were busy drawing pictures. As the teacher walked around the tables, she asked one of the boys named Harry, what he was drawing.

"I am drawing God!" he replied.
"You can't draw God ... nobody knows what he looks like!" exclaimed the teacher.
"They will after I finish!" replied Harry.

As children, we do not let other people's opinions (and even accepted facts) influence our actions. Unfortunately, as we grow up, we become very dependent on what others think—on what is considered right and what is considered wrong. Many of us even choose our careers and our life partners depending on how they will be accepted by everyone around us.

I say, you only have one life to live – *your* life! Do not let human dependency for approval and acceptance affect you. Do not settle for a comfortable existence when you deserve a wonderful life of purpose and fulfilment!

# Action Steps

1. What can you do to live a life of purpose and fulfilment? Just one thing: commit to yourself (if you haven't done so yet) that you will not settle for anything less than that.
2. When you allow yourself to be who you are, you automatically allow others to be who they are.
3. You can give this gift of personal freedom to yourself and others. All you need is the courage to live your life on your terms!

# It All Comes Down to Faith

Someone once told me that if you have $100,000 in the bank, then no one ever tells you how to live your life! Well, maybe some people still tell you, but it is done on a different level and not as often as if you were struggling financially. Why is success mainly measured by how much money you have? It is no wonder that so many people give up on their dreams in pursuit of financial stability and approval from others!

No one likes to be told what to do and how to do it. We like the approval of others, especially our loved ones, so we give up on what is important to us and become part of the masses, doing "what works," what's been done before, and what more or less guarantees a paycheck.

Often there is money in your bank account, but what about your heart? Is it content? Is it full of life and passion, full of love and appreciation, full of anticipation of what the next day will bring? Is the next day of your life truly *yours*?

Do not misunderstand me; there is nothing wrong with wanting to have money and striving for financial stability. In fact, it is an important part of your overall success. The point I am making is that, while working on creating wealth, remember to take care of all your other needs as well.

In order to have something that you do not currently have in your life, you first have to become the kind of person who attracts whatever they want into their lives—the kind of partner that you want, wealth, certain types of friends, a healthy body, or just peace of mind.

Yes, at times, it seems like a very slow process. We all want results *now*; we want immediate gratification. We want what can be measured with our physical senses.

So what is the solution? Well, it all comes down to *faith*. To live the life of your dreams – the life that is truly *yours* – it is essential to have faith in your dreams, in yourself, and in the universe!

# Action Steps

1. When you know exactly what you want, do all that you can to become the kind of person who will attract it. If you are looking for a fulfilling relationship, immerse yourself in the information and thoughts on what makes such a relationship possible.
2. The same goes for wealth. To attract wealth, raise your "wealth conscience" — study money, read about money, and find out what wealthy people think about and do when it comes to money. Before you know it, great people, wealth, health, and everything else you constantly focus on will manifest into your life and *stay* there!

PART 2

THE SECRETS OF PEOPLE WHO ARE SUCCESSFUL

# What Successful People Know

*The successful person makes a habit of doing what the failing person doesn't like to do.*
   —**Thomas Edison** (1847–1931, American inventor and businessman)

What do successful people know, think, believe, and do, that the rest do not? What are the secrets of people who are successful?

Fortunately, there are no secrets! There is a certain set of beliefs and habits and a particular attitude of mind that anyone can learn and make his own — in the process, *attracting* success in all areas of his life. I have studied success and successful people for many years and have concluded that some of the aspects they have in common are the following:

- They know what they want!
- They are usually very passionate about what they do.
- They have clear visions as to where they are going.
- They have clearly defined values by which they live and base their decisions.
- They have powerful winning habits.
- They have a positive outlook on life.
- They ask many questions and enjoy learning.
- Time is their most valuable commodity, and they spend it wisely.
- They understand and accept themselves as they are.

# Action Steps

If you haven't done so already, start a success journal. Every night, before you go to sleep, write down the answers to the following three questions:

1. What am I grateful for today?
2. What new empowering things did I learn today?
3. What exciting new ideas do I have?

Every morning, start your day with reading the previous night's entries in your success journal. Then, add to it your goals for the day. And remember, the main thing that separates successful people from the rest is that they actually take action rather than just reading or thinking about taking it!

# What Is Success?

Are you rushing through your days, working hard to achieve *your* success or *someone else's*? Sometimes we are on autopilot, doing things because we feel we have to, because we feel it is our duty, yet, not really going anywhere ...

Here is a story that might inspire you to stop and think about what you *really* want:

A young fisherman was lying in his boat on a lazy Sunday afternoon, enjoying the sun and the stillness around him. Suddenly, his boat started to move, and the noise of a much bigger boat approaching took him out of his daydream. He looked up and heard a wealthy-looking man, who was the owner of the boat, greeting him. After a short conversation, the wealthy businessman decided to give the young fisherman some advice on running a successful business.

"Today is your lucky day!" he said excitedly to the young fisherman. "I am going to teach you how to become very successful!" The young man stretched his arms lazily and made himself comfortable.

A little taken aback by the lack of the young fisherman's enthusiasm, the wealthy businessmen continued anyway. "If you work extra time, you can put the money aside to buy yourself another little boat. Then you can hire someone to help you and eventually buy two more little boats."

"Why would I want to do that?" asked the young fisherman, unimpressed.

Getting irritated, the wealthy man continued, "Because then you can get yourself a bigger boat, like mine, and make lots and lots of money!"

"And why would I want to do that?" asked the young fisherman, stretching his legs.

Hardly containing himself, the wealthy businessman exclaimed, "Because then you will be wealthy, and you don't have to work anymore — you can do what you like, relax in the sun, and enjoy your life!"

The young fisherman smiled wisely, closed his eyes as he lay down once again, and said, "Ah, that sounds wonderful!"

## Action Steps

1. Ask yourself: "Am I successful?" If yes, then "What makes me successful?" If no, then "What is missing in my life that would make me feel successful?" Remember, success is just a *feeling*, and it is up to you to decide what you need to do to experience that feeling, or under what circumstances you will *allow* yourself to experience the feeling of success.
2. Here is another secret of successful people: first, *feel* successful, and then success will follow!

# One Word to Define Success

*Success isn't something you chase. It is something you have to put forth the effort for constantly; then maybe it'll come when you least expect it.*
> **—Michael Jordan** (professional basketball player)

A great attitude is not the result of success; success is the result of a great attitude.
—**Earl Nightingale** (1921–1989, entrepreneur, producer, and publisher)

Can you define success? If you could use just one word to define success, what would it be?

When I ask my workshop participants and my coaching clients to define success, the answers are usually different. So the one word that I would use to describe success is *personal* – it means different things to different people.

Here is my definition of success:
I feel successful when I live my days consistent with my values, take action steps towards my goals and dreams, and when I make a difference in someone's life. I also believe that the ultimate measure of success is how good you feel about yourself on a regular basis!

I once asked one of my clients, world famous Poker Champion Paul Zimbler, what his definition of success was, and here is what he shared with me:

Success is achieving the best you can do,
Being honest, committed, hardworking, and true.
Don't dwell in the past, look forward, not back.
Give yourself chances others will lack.

Anyone can make mistakes on the way.
Success is learning that errors can pay.
Dream without limit, plan without fear.
Before you expect it, the future is here.

Reach for the sky, aim for the sun,
Achievers will finish a job once begun.

## Action Steps

1. Write down your own definition of success. Unless you are very clear about what you are striving to achieve, how can you know when you've achieved it?
2. Find out what success means to the important people in your life. It will help you to understand them better and assist them in achieving it.

# What Determines Success?

*For every difficulty that supposedly stops a person from succeeding, there are thousands who have had it a lot worse and have succeeded anyway. So can you.*

—**Brian Tracy** (self-development guru and author)

Are people predisposed to be successful, or is it learnable? Let me share with you examples from history about people who didn't start as well as they finished.

One of the most influential figures of our millennium, Thomas Edison, didn't learn to talk until the age of four, had a learning disorder, and, later on in his life, said, *"My father thought I was stupid, and I almost decided I must be a dunce."*

Albert Einstein, whose name and image have become a representation of supernormal intelligence, was dyslexic and very slow developmentally as a child. His Greek teacher told him "You will never amount to anything." He was expelled from high school and failed his college entrance exam.

French, post-Impressionist painter Paul Gauguin, who helped form the basis of modern art, only began painting because he failed as a stockbroker.

The renowned French mathematical physicist Henri Poincare did very poorly on his IQ test and was proclaimed an "imbecile."

Rodgers and Hammerstein's first collaboration was so disastrous that they didn't work again for years. (They both went on to create several outstanding musical productions.)

Walt Disney was fired by a newspaper editor because he lacked "good creative ideas."

Beethoven's music teacher told him he was "hopeless as a composer."

So what determines success? It is your mindset—your set of beliefs and views about yourself and about life, that are, fortunately, both learnable and changeable.

## Action Steps

1. To be successful, you need to study success and what successful people do – their mindsets. In neuro-linguistic programming terms, it is called "modeling." Start noticing people around you who are successful, as well as people who are famous for their success. What determines *their* success? What determines *your* success?
2. The more you think and analyze success, the more of it you will attract in your life—because what you focus on is what you get.

# Can You Really Change Your Life in One Minute?

*Some day, in years to come, you will be wrestling with the great temptation, or trembling under the great sorrow of your life. But the real struggle is here, now, in these quiet weeks. Now it is being decided whether, in the day of your supreme sorrow or temptation, you shall miserably fail or gloriously conquer. Character cannot be made except by a steady, long, continued process.*

**—Phillips Brooks** (1835–1893, American Episcopal bishop)

I call myself *The One Minute Coach* for two reasons:

1. People seek quick results (immediate gratification), and they are just too busy taking care of life's daily demands to spend too much time on self-improvement.
2. I really do believe that we *can* change our lives in one minute, and here is why …

How does change happen?

Your life changes the instant you make a decision to change. So, in reality, it takes even less than a minute to make the change that you want to make; however, you need many minutes to accumulate the information that leads to a particular decision. It is like a puzzle that needs enough pieces to see the whole picture.

Many people get frustrated that, no matter how hard they try, no matter how many books they read or seminars they attend, they still don't seem to achieve what they want. Unfortunately, many people give up on living their dream lives …

If you feel frustrated with the lack of change or progress in your life, you should relax and have faith that what you are doing right now is accumulating the "pieces of the puzzle" that, when the time is right, will lead you to make the changes that you desire.

# Action Steps

1. *Never* give up! You might be just one little piece away from getting what you want. Realize that sometimes it takes twenty years to achieve an overnight success!
2. Keep learning and growing. By changing who you are, you inevitably change your experiences and your life.
3. *Take action!* However small it is, if it moves you in the right direction, just do it. If you have a dream, take at least one action step towards it in the next half hour – it will make you feel empowered and in control.
4. Then, do something every day, keep your eyes on the destination, and you *will* get there!

# Do Not Underestimate Your Skills

Do you know what you are worth? Most people tend to underestimate their skills and undercharge their services. The following is a parable that I believe we can all learn from:

During the height of the crab fishing season off the coast of Alaska, a young captain and his crew were busy preparing their ship to set sail in what is the most dangerous, yet most profitable, fishing season in the world.

After hours of exhaustive preparation, the ship was finally ready to embark on its first season ever. As the crew waited anxiously on deck for the captain to fire up the engines, they realized, after several minutes of complete silence, that something was wrong. What had started off as an exciting morning was quickly turning into a nightmare, with all the crew members in the engine room trying to figure out what the problem was.

After several hours of failed attempts, the captain and his crew surfaced back on deck and, not being able to get any help at that hour, they made their way through the empty port to the local bar. As the captain sat at the bar, he started explaining to an old sailor sitting next to him, the horror of his situation.

"I can fix it for you," said the old sailor. "But it wont be cheap ... $10,000 is my fee!"

"No problem," replied the captain, immediately realizing that this was a small fee, compared to missing the whole season.

As the captain and the old sailor made their way down to the engine room, the old sailor picked up a hammer from the floor and started looking over the engine. After about thirty seconds, he hit something three times and told the captain to fire up the engines.

Immediately, the engines started, and the old man made his way back on deck to collect his fee, at which point the young captain started questioning the old man about how he could possibly imagine getting paid $10,000 for just hitting the engines a few times. The old man simply smiled and said, "I will write you an invoice that will outline the fee."

The captain opened the folded piece of paper that the old sailor handed to him and read:

Hitting the engine three times....................................$1
Knowing where to hit......................................... $9,999

The captain smiled understandingly and paid the old sailor the full amount.

## Action Steps

1. Remember, you are a unique human being with a unique combination of skills, knowledge, and experience that no one else possesses.
2. You can never earn in the outside world more than you can earn in your own mind. If you want to earn more money, then first become very comfortable with the new sum in your mind, and then you will be able to attract it into your life.
3. Know your worth, and others will do the same in return.

# The Most Important Ingredient for Your Success

*Calm self-confidence is as far from conceit as the desire to earn a decent living is remote from greed.*

—**Channing Pollock** (1880–1946, American playwright, critic, and writer)

*To have that sense of one's intrinsic worth which constitutes self-respect is potentially to have everything.*

—**Joan Didion** (American essayist, journalist, and novelist)

What would you say is the most important ingredient for overall success? I believe it is self-confidence and a high level of self-esteem. You can only achieve your goals and attract success when you feel you deserve to have, to do, or to be what you want. You feel you deserve it all when your self-esteem is high.

The formula is simple: raise your self-esteem, and a new level of success follows! To have more confidence and self-esteem within days, just follow the five action steps below.

# Action Steps

1. Anthony Robbins, an achievement guru, suggests you stop analyzing yourself and focus on how you can contribute to others.

2. He also encourages controlling your mental focus. The fastest way to change what you're focusing on, says Robbins, is to change the questions you're asking yourself. For example, change questions such as "What happens if I fail at this?" or "Why do I always screw these things up?" to "What's the best way to get this done now?" or, better yet, "What's the best way to get this done and enjoy the process?"

3. Change your core beliefs. Change from "I've never done it before so I don't see how I could do it today" to "If I can imagine it, I can achieve it!"

4. Recall five of your greatest successes, and write a paragraph in your success journal describing each one. Use these examples to remind yourself that you can always find a way!

5. Take good care of yourself regularly. Because, when you take care of yourself – your growth, happiness, and self-fulfilment – you inevitably take care of the world and the people around you – their happiness and their future!

PART 3

WHY DO WE SUFFER?

# Are You Looking For Problems?

*We suffer less when we let go of planning ahead to feel poorly.*

**—Hale Dwoskin**

I believe that most of our suffering is caused by our own perceptions! In his best-selling book, *The Sedona Method*, Hale Dwoskin points out that "the reason problems appear to persist through time, is that whenever they're not here in this moment, we go looking for them."

Most of the time when you are suffering, you are not actually experiencing anything negative at that moment except the *memory* of something that has caused you grief or a vision of something that might happen (worrying). Your thoughts are either on your past, which is not real at this moment, or in the future, which is also not real at this moment.

This leads to the conclusion that suffering is your choice! Here is a story that will demonstrate my point.

Two monks were heading back to their temple after a long journey through the mountains of Tibet. Suddenly, they noticed a young woman lying by the riverbed, injured with a strained ankle and unable to get home. Immediately, the older monk went to the woman and inquired if he could help. He then lifted her up and carried her back to the safety of her village.

Completely confused and angry, the younger monk silently walked behind. After the woman was left safely with her relatives, the two monks were back on their journey to the temple.

Furious, the young monk kept thinking to himself, "How could he do that? How could he break the vow of chastity and hold her in his arms? How could he even speak to her?"

After several minutes, the young monk could not hold it in any longer and approached the older monk, "How could you do that? How could you pay so little regard to your vows?"

Surprised, the older monk looked kindly into the younger monk's eyes and said, "I am no longer carrying her, my brother. Are you?"

## Action Steps

1. Every time you want to analyze a problem, think of it as if it were in the *past*. Do not try to understand why it happened to you unless you are planning to experience it again in the future.
2. Remember, whatever you focus on is what you get again and again and again. Instead of focusing on what is wrong and why, focus on what is right and on what you *want* to experience today and in the future.

# How to Get What You Want

*The greatest discovery of my generation is that human beings can alter their lives by altering their attitudes of mind.*
> —**William James** (1842–1910, pioneering American psychologist and philosopher)

*You have powers you never dreamed of. You can do things you never thought you could do. There are no limitations in what you can do except the limitations of your own mind.*
> —**Darwin P. Kingsley** (1906–1930, American business leader)

Have you ever found yourself wondering why someone who is not as smart, not as good-looking, not as creative, not as connected, not nearly as "good a person" as you, seems to have it all … while you, who seems to give, give, give, and do, do, do, are still struggling? Or maybe you heard someone else say that?

The answer is simple: what one person possesses and the other doesn't, has nothing to do with what that person has or does … it concerns that person's *mindset*. The mindset is the belief system that people operate with — determining what they experience, what they do, what they have, and who they are.

For you to attract money, good health, loving relationships, or anything else you desire, you have to develop a mindset that will allow your desires to flow freely into your life.

# Action Steps

1. The best way to develop a mindset that allows you to have what you want is to study the mindsets of people who already have what you want.
2. Changing your thoughts and beliefs changes your life! Be positive, optimistic, and grateful. Rather than worry and attract negative events, project into the future what you *want* to experience.
3. Be *harmonious* congruent. Align all your thoughts, beliefs, and actions in the direction you want to go. For example, if you want to be wealthy but think that money is dirty or that rich people are selfish, then you are not congruent.
4. Finally, know deep in your heart that you deserve to have all that your heart desires! Be comfortable with having it in your mind first, and the reality will follow shortly.

# An Opportunity for Guaranteed Enlightenment

*You gain strength, courage, and confidence by every experience in which you really stop to look fear in the face. You must do the thing you think you cannot do.*

—**Eleanor Roosevelt** (1884–1962, former American First Lady)

*Courage is not the absence of fear, but rather the judgment that something else is more important than one's fear.*

—**Ambrose Redmoon** (1933–1996, American writer and rock music manager)

What is your greatest fear? Are you ready to let it go? The best way to overcome fears is to do the things you fear.

There is a story that in ancient Tibet all the monks would gather together once every hundred years and be given an opportunity for guaranteed enlightenment — all they had to do was walk through the *Tunnel of Fear*.

Those monks who would gather up their courage and step into the darkness of the tunnel would be faced with their worst and biggest fears – snakes, spiders, unexpected heights, closed-in spaces, as well as painful feelings of loneliness, deceit, injustice, and powerlessness. Whatever they feared was guaranteed to show up in that tunnel.

There was one rule that the monks had to follow in order to come out of the tunnel and receive enlightenment: no matter what they heard, saw, or felt, they had to keep walking.

The hardest part about overcoming your fears is making that first step. Then, all you have to do is to keep moving. The rewards for facing your fears are happiness, success, and enlightenment.

# Action Steps

1. Identify something you've wanted to do for a long time but feel too afraid to do—something that you keep postponing, finding good reasons for not doing, yet all the time you get that feeling in your gut that this is something that needs to be done. It could be calling someone, sharing something, speaking in public, leaving your job, starting a new career … *you know* what it is!
2. Remember, nothing comes without a price, and the price for not doing what needs to be done is much higher than actually doing it!
3. Identify what it is you fear, and just do it. Your courage will liberate, empower, and enlighten you!

# Success Is Not Forever, and Failure Is Not Fatal

*Don't get a big head when you win or get too down in the dumps when you lose. Keep things in perspective. Success is not forever, and failure isn't fatal.*

**—Don Shula** (NFL coach)

How do you stay levelheaded and calm when stress (both positive and negative) seems to be a constant in your life?

To answer this question, I would first point out that a certain level of stress is actually good for you; it is when it gets out of hand that it starts interfering with the way you function and how you react to this world. When your energies are channeled into mulling over what happened in the past or into stressing out about the future, you cannot produce the kind of results you are capable of producing.

So what is the solution?

Don Shula, who is described as the most winning coach in NFL history, had a twenty-four-hour rule to deal with the stresses of winning or losing a game. He allowed himself and his players a maximum of twenty-four hours after a football game to celebrate a victory or grief over a defeat. During that time, everyone was encouraged to experience the thrill of victory or the agony of defeat as deeply as possible, while learning as much as they could from that experience.

Once the twenty-four-hour deadline had passed, they put the game behind them and focused their energies on preparing for the next opponent.

# Action Steps

The next time you find yourself filled with despair over loss or failure or celebrating a great achievement, apply Shula's twenty-four-hour rule — give yourself a twenty-four-hour deadline to deal with it, and then get on with your life.

By the way, Hall of Fame Coach Shula is the only coach to guide a team (the Miami Dolphins) through an undefeated NFL season (17–0 in 1972)! Who knows — maybe applying his rule will help *you* have an undefeated life! And if it doesn't … well, you have twenty-four hours to get over it!

# How Successful People Deal with Failure

What is failure? Is failure the opposite of success? Do you believe in failure? How do you feel about failure? How we feel about failure is greatly related to how successful we become.

I personally do not believe in failure. I believe that the only way I can fail is by giving up! It is okay for me to make mistakes and to fall down sometimes. In fact, it indicates to me that I try and take risks. It is when I choose to stay down that I would consider myself a failure.

I came to this empowering belief because I learnt from people I admire. Today I want you to think about failure and analyze how other people we hold in our esteem and consider to be successful, have dealt or still deal with failure:

*I feel that the most important requirement in success is learning to overcome failure. You must learn to tolerate it, but never accept it.*
> **—Reggie Jackson** (member of the Baseball Hall of Fame)

*A man's life is interesting primarily when he had failed—for it's a sign that he tried to surpass himself.*
> **—Georges Clemenceau** (1841–1929, French statesman, physician, and journalist)

*A man can get discouraged many times, but he is not a failure until he begins to blame somebody else and stops trying.*
> **—John Burroughs** (1837–1921, American naturalist and essayist)

*If you don't fail now and again, it's a sign you're playing it safe.*
> **—Woody Allen** (Academy Award winning American film director, writer, actor, musician, and comedian)

*My great concern is not whether you have failed, but whether you are content with your failure.*
> **—Abraham Lincoln** (1809–1865, sixteenth president of the United States)

*The only man who never makes mistakes is the man who never does anything.*
—**Theodore Roosevelt** (1858–1919, twenty-sixth president of the United States)

*The men who try to do something and fail are infinitely better than those who try to do nothing and succeed.*
—**Martin Lloyd Jones** (1899–1981, Welsh theologian)

*He's no failure. He's not dead yet.*
—**William Lloyd George** (1879–1941, 1st Baron Lloyd of Dolobran, UK)

## Action Steps

1. If you find yourself feeling like a failure, then go back to this page and read the quotes again.
2. Realize that, although you might not always control what happens to you, you are always in control of how you *react* to it.
3. Create your own empowering belief about ""failure," and then use it for yourself and share it with others.

# Are You Guilty?

*Lack of forgiveness causes almost all of our self-sabotaging behavior.*
—**Mark Victor Hansen** (American motivational speaker,
trainer, and author)

Let's talk about *guilt* and *shame* – feelings that cause us unnecessary suffering, often make us ill, deplete our energies, and prevent us from being happy and having peace of mind.

First, realize that feelings of guilt and shame are self-infused. According to Hale Dwoskin, author of one of my favourite books *The Sedona Method*, "*guilt* is the feeling of remorse that follows a perceived wrongdoing; *shame* is a painful emotion resulting from an awareness of inadequacy or guilt. While it is possible to feel guilt without shame, we cannot feel shame without guilt."

Don't let any one make you feel guilty! Including, or should I say, especially, yourself!

Negative people with low-self esteem tend to try to make others feel guilty to give themselves a false sense of superiority. In reality, it only contributes more to their low self-esteem.

Remember, nobody can make you feel anything unless you let him or her make you feel that way! Guilt and shame do nothing except make what you did worse for yourself and others.

# Action Steps

1. Forgive yourself. You are not a bad person because you did something that made you feel guilty. If you were a bad person, then you wouldn't feel guilty about it.

2. Realize that feeling guilty or shameful is your way of punishing yourself for what you did or thinking that it will prevent future recurrence of the event. Nothing can be further from reality because, by holding in your mind and constantly replaying the event that made you feel guilty, you make it a lot more possible to happen again.

3. Remember, what we visualize and think about, we manifest. In the end, we never feel as though we've been sufficiently punished anyway. If you've been holding onto feelings of guilt or shame, it is time to let go of these destructive feelings. They are just feelings; they are not who you are. Learn from them, let them go, and move on!

4. If you made a mistake, acknowledge it, apologize for it, learn from it, let go, and be happy! It is your right!

# Eliminating Worry

*Worry does not empty tomorrow of sorrow—it empties today of strength.*
> **—Carrie Ten Bloom** (best-selling author)

*When I look back on all these worries, I remember the story of the old man who said on his deathbed that he had a lot of trouble in his life, most of which had never happened.*
> **—Sir Winston Churchill** (1874–1965, UK prime minister)

*The reason why worry kills more people than work is that more people worry than work.*
> **—Robert Frost** (1875–1963, American poet)

*Stop the mindless wishing that things would be different. Rather than wasting time and emotional and spiritual energy in explaining why we don't have what we want, we can start to pursue other ways to get it.*
> **—Greg Anderson** (American writer and cancer survivor)

One of the worst energy and time wasters – *worry* – is a big part of many people's lives. Ask yourself:

- Do I worry a lot?
- What happens when I worry?
- What is worrying me?

Worrying is a process of thinking and visualizing an undesirable outcome. Most likely, you already know that it is a dangerous process, since we don't want to focus on what we don't want to experience. So what to do? Follow the two simple steps outlined below.

# Action Steps

1. To eliminate worry, first identify the worst possible outcome of any particular situation, and decide how you would deal with it.
2. Then, quickly change the image to exactly what you *want* to happen, and keep *that* image in your head.

# Why Do We Argue?

If you have ever tried unsuccessfully to convince someone of something that made perfect sense to you but not to that person, it is because of the difference in your belief systems.

Here is an interesting story told by the legendary psychologist, Abraham Maslow:

> A psychiatrist was treating a patient who believed that he was a corpse. The psychiatrist used every cognitive approach to convince the man that he was indeed alive, all to no avail.
>
> In a moment of revelation, the psychiatrist asked the man, "Do you believe that corpses bleed?" The patient replied, "That's ridiculous! Of course, corpses don't bleed."
>
> After asking permission, the psychiatrist pricked the patient's finger, producing a drop of red blood. At that moment, the psychiatrist thought that a moment of enlightenment was forthcoming. However, the patient looked at his finger with astonishment and exclaimed, "I'll be damned; corpses do bleed!"

Your beliefs shape your experiences and the way you see the world. They determine how you make decisions, how you feel about things, how you react to things, and, ultimately, they determine the direction you take in life.

Imagine you are in a tall tower with millions of windows that have very different views. Your beliefs will determine through which window you will choose to view the world outside.

This is not just important in understanding why and how you experience *your* life, but also in understanding that different people sit at different windows and view different things. What is true to you from your window might not be true from another person's perspective.

## Action Steps

1. Keep the above in mind next time someone is trying to force his or her point of view on you. Think of the difference in perspective next time you are trying to force your viewpoint onto someone else.
2. Unless you are willing to adopt or understand each other's belief systems and look at the situation at hand from "the same window," you will just get frustrated trying to understand something that doesn't exist in your window of perceptions.

# How to Eliminate Self-Sabotaging Beliefs

*Our only limitations are those which we set up in our minds or permit others to establish for us.*

—**Elizabeth Arden** (1878–1966, Canadian businesswoman)

Let's talk about what is probably **your worst enemy** when it comes to success — *self-sabotage*.

According to Anthony Robbins, a leading authority on self-development and peak performance, "Anything we do, including self-sabotage, we do with **positive intent**." That means that our brain is always trying to benefit us through its actions — whether we are conscious about it or not.

If you find yourself still struggling to achieve your ideal weight, accumulate wealth, fall in love with "the right person," quit smoking, travel to that special place you always wanted to go, or any other goal you are still hoping to reach, then realize that you have not achieved it because your brain is trying to protect you.

For example, if you have a fear of failure or a fear of success, or if you have a fear of commitment or a fear of being rejected, then you will subconsciously sabotage any chances of achieving your goal that might put you in the position where you will have to face your fears!

I believe we all have fears and self-sabotaging beliefs in certain areas of our lives — it might be money, relationships, weight issues, or success in general.

*Why* we sabotage ourselves is not as important to understand (you might spend years trying to find out, and it will only cause low self-esteem) as learning *how* to face your fears and eliminate self-sabotaging beliefs.

# Action Steps

1. Identify in what areas of your life you might be sabotaging yourself.
2. Do everything in your power to feel good, because your brain is trying to help you avoid pain and gain pleasure.
3. The only way to eliminate fear is by *doing* what you fear.
4. Interrupt the old pattern. Rehearse achieving the success you want, and feel the pleasure of succeeding, until it becomes your new empowering habit.

# Everything Is Relative

When you think one situation is bad, that is because you are comparing it to something that you perceive is better. Let's look at this example:

Imagine you have a daughter who recently left for college. This is the first time she has gone away, and she is only eighteen years old. You have not heard from her in a while, and finally a letter arrives:

*Dear Mum and Dad,*

*I have been very busy and would like to fill you in on some exciting developments in my life.*

*Three weeks ago I met a wonderful man, John. After failing my math exam and dropping out of college, we rode to Las Vegas on a motorcycle and got married. It was so romantic; we even got matching tattoos! John is from a great family, and I am sure you will approve of my decision.*

*You will be even more excited when I tell you that you will be grandparents soon! I plan on visiting you when the baby is born, and I am looking forward to it! Got to run now, but promise to write again soon.*

*Your loving daughter,*
*Jessica*

*PS: Actually, I did not drop out of college; I did not get married, and I am not pregnant, but I did fail the math exam and was hoping this letter will help you see it from a better perspective!*

When my six-year-old daughter lost a pair of white shoes at the pool, she optimistically came to me and said, "Isn't it great, Mommy, that I didn't lose my pink shoes as well?"

Most young children have an inborn sense of optimism and positive expectations in life. That is because they haven't yet learned how to be negative.

I believe that things can always be better, and they can always be worse, but whatever happens to us at this moment is exactly what should happen, and it is for the best!

## Action Step

Make a conscious effort to enjoy each moment, stay positive, and expect the best in life. Before you know it, it will become another one of your positive habits!

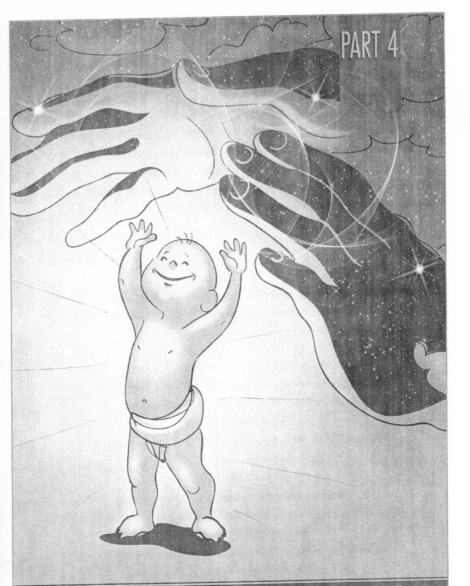

# PART 4

# THE SECRET TO A GREAT LIFE

# Who Are You Not to Be?

*When one door of happiness closes, another opens; but often we look so long at the closed door that we do not see the one which has been opened for us.*
—**Helen Keller** (1880–1968, deaf, blind American author, activist, and lecturer)

It is amazing how many people feel they don't deserve to be happy, don't deserve to have the best, don't deserve to *be* the best, or don't deserve to have it all! Many settle for second best, and many get stuck in the comfort zone, in the familiar. They don't want to "rock the boat." Second best plus security is a lot more important to them than going for the life of their dreams.

Why?

To answer this question, let me share with you one of my favourite poems by Marianne Williamson, from her book *A Return to Love: Reflections on the Principles of A Course in Miracles.*

> Our deepest fear is not that we are inadequate.
> Our deepest fear is that we are powerful beyond measure.
> It is our light, not our darkness, that most frightens us.
> We ask ourselves:
> Who am I to be brilliant, gorgeous, talented, and fabulous?
> Actually who are you not to be?
> You are a child of God.
> Your playing small doesn't serve the world.
> There is nothing enlightened about shrinking so that other people won't feel insecure around you.
> We are born to manifest the glory of God that is within us.
> It is not just in some of us; it's in everyone.
> And as we let our own light shine, we unconsciously give other people permission to do the same.
> As we are liberated from our own fear our presence automatically liberates others.

# Action Steps

1. Make a decision today, that you deserve to live your life in a way that makes *you* happy. The rewards for this one decision are greater than you could ever imagine!
2. Choose today and for the rest of your life not to settle for second best because it is convenient, comfortable, or secure. If you do that, then you might always wonder where you could have ended up if you really did go for your dreams!

# Life Is about Creating Yourself

*Life isn't about finding yourself.* **Life is about creating yourself.**
—**George Bernard Shaw** (1856–1950, Irish playwright and
Nobel Prize winner in literature)

*Remember, happiness doesn't depend upon who you are or what you have;
it depends solely upon what you think.*
—**Dale Carnegie** (1888–1955, American author and speaker)

*No one is in control of your happiness but you. Therefore, you have the power
to change anything about yourself or your life that you want to change.*
—**Barbara De Angelis** (relationship guru and best-selling author)

Did you know that your brain can hold only *one* bit of information in any
given moment? This is a very important fact.

Why?

Because if you are focusing on something negative and unpleasant, then
everything positive that you are experiencing in your life is lost at that
moment. And there is always something positive in your life, if you only
look for it. It is *your* choice!

# Action Steps

Next time you catch yourself thinking a negative thought or picturing a negative outcome … *stop!* Erase that negative thought and that picture, and replace it with what you *want* to happen. Here are some ways to do it:

1. Mentally delete the unwanted information, as if it were on a computer screen. See the blank page, and design a positive picture for the desired outcome.
2. Imagine the image is on a regular piece of paper. See yourself as you tear that paper into tiny little pieces. Then, take out a new paper, and paint a new image.
3. Another approach is to rewind the "old message" or the memory of what has happened and then record a new, more positive version over it.

Eventually, you will discover your own personal way of replacing negative thoughts and visions with positive ones that work best for you.

# What Does It Take to Be Attractive?

All around me, I see people rushing to buy beautiful clothes, going to the hairdressers, and paying for manicures and pedicures, facials, and makeup — all in the desire to look attractive for that special party or date. I also notice that very few people focus on the most important aspect of beauty – the beauty within!

How many times have you seen a person with a strikingly beautiful face and body, but who is not "attractive" at all (often after you start speaking with them)? And other times you will meet someone who is not "really beautiful," yet you feel totally attracted to that person. He or she might not even "be your type," but you still find the person very attractive. Why?

Being attractive comes from having that magnetic power that pulls people towards you. A power that inspires others to talk to you and find out more about who you are. A power that makes others want to be like you!

# Action Steps

1. Feel good about how you look. It is good and healthy to want to look beautiful and spend time working on it. When you look good, you feel good, and that adds to your inner attraction.

2. Feel good about who you are as a person. Work on your self-esteem. Be confident in your own skin. *Confidence* is the greatest attraction of all! To have that, only think good things about yourself, and do affirmations such as "I like myself," "I am very attractive," and "I allow myself to be liked and admired for who I am."

3. If you want others to like you, like *them* first. Be careful of what you are thinking. What you think and feel is communicated to others subliminally. Compliment someone whom you like in your mind, and see how attractive he or she will find *you*!

4. *Smile*! It is easy to do and easy not to, but a smile adds tremendously to your attractiveness.

5. Finally, focus on who you are and not just on what you look like. People fall in love with the essence of you – your energy, the sparkle in your eyes, your passion for living, your unconditional love – everything that makes you unique and special. People fall in love with your beautiful soul!

# How Much Do You Love Yourself?

Let's talk about *love*. More specifically, I would like to focus on self-love.

Why?

Because you cannot give more than you have — in order to give and receive love, you have to first love yourself. According to the last statement, then it is logical to conclude that we are capable of giving love in direct proportion to how much we actually love and like ourselves.

Moreover, what if we allowed others to love and like us in direct proportion to how much we love and like ourselves?

# Action Steps

1. Think about how your past and current relationships have been affected due to the information above. If you have had negative experiences with love and feel you might have sabotaged yourself in the past, maybe it is because you feel you do not deserve to be loved.
2. Decide today (or as soon as you are ready) that you deserve to be loved *for who you are*! You do not need to prove your worth to anyone. Think about a newborn baby who is loved unconditionally from the minute he or she is born.
3. Forgive yourself for past mistakes, and accept yourself with all your wonderful imperfections as well as your unique talents. Love yourself for who you are, and the world will love you in return!

# Have a Great Day!

*I never ran 1000 miles. I could never have done that. I ran one mile 1000 times.*

—**Stu Mittleman** (world record holder for ultra-distance running)

And in the end, it's not the years in your life that count. It's the life in your years.

—**Abraham Lincoln**

What is the secret to having a great life? Well, if you had to divide life into measurable bits, you could start with years. So, to have a great life, you would have to start by first having a set of great years, one after another.

You could then divide years into months. Therefore, to have a great year, you would focus on having a great twelve months (one month at a time). To have a great month, you would need to have four great weeks. To have a great week, all you have to do is just focus on having seven great days.

My conclusion? To have a great life, ultimately you have to have a *great day!* *One day at a time.*

This simple conclusion has changed my life! I value every day to the fullest and do my best to make it as successful, productive, and happy as I can. Every single day represents life to me, because that is what life is made of – days, hours, minutes, seconds, moments …

If you look at each moment as a precious part of *your* life and live it to the fullest, you will be very happy and fulfilled indeed!

# Action Step

Value and make the best of each day, each hour, and each minute of your life. Be conscious that once that time is gone, it is gone forever …

PART 5

ARE YOU A NATURAL LEADER?

# Leadership Begins With You

*The greatest privilege of leadership is the chance to elevate lives.*
—**Robin Sharma** (best-selling author of *The Monk Who Sold His Ferrari*)

Are great leaders born or made? What does it mean to be a great leader?

In a society of hierarchies, it is often assumed that CEOs, company owners, and other people in positions of power are the leaders. In fact, position has nothing to do with it! One can be in charge of hundreds of people and not be a leader at all. At the same time, someone without a management or leadership position can be a great leader. Are you?

Leadership is not about position. Leadership is about inspiring, motivating, and influencing others to follow your cause. It's about passion. It's about action. It's about having great dreams and then doing all it takes to manifest them.

Leadership is not about managing people but about guiding and motivating them. A great leader is someone who allows and encourages others to develop their highest potential, express their individuality, and honor their own lives.

# Action Steps

1. Great leadership begins within *you*. You cannot be a great leader of other lives before you can effectively lead your own. Ask yourself:

- What am I passionate about?
- Do I have a compelling vision that inspires and motivates me?
- Do I have the discipline that helps me make the right choices and take action steps that bring me closer to my vision?
- Do I understand the values that drive me, and do I live by them?
- Do I honor my own life, and am I true to myself?
- Do I allow myself to express my highest potential and believe that I am here to make a difference?

2. Remember, you are unique and have something to offer to this world that no one else has. Have the courage to unleash your genius, and be the light that others want to follow.

# The Power of a Team and Cooperation

Most of my work is focused on researching and understanding what makes some people more successful than others — understanding the mindset behind success. One thing successful people recognize and maximize is the power of a good team.

I once heard a story of a man who died and went to Heaven. As he entered the gates of Heaven, God asked him, "Do you have any final wishes before you spend the rest of eternity in Heaven?" The man replied, "Yes, I'd like to see what Hell is like, so that I can fully appreciate Heaven."

Instantaneously God granted his wish, and they found themselves in Hell. The man witnessed the most unusual scene. There was a long banquet table with an abundance of delicious looking food; yet, the people who were sitting on both sides of the table seemed grumpy, miserable, and very hungry.

"Why do these people look so hungry and unhappy, with all this food around them?" asked the man. God replied, "Because they can only use ten-foot chopsticks to eat from the table." The man felt sorry for the people and was ready to go back to Heaven.

Upon entering Heaven, the man noticed a very similar scene, with a long table piled high with delicious food; however, the people around that table seemed completely satisfied and happy!

"Wow, what a difference!" said the man. "I guess in Heaven people are allowed to use knives and forks?" "No" replied God. "In Heaven, we also use ten-foot chopsticks" Completely confused, the man asked, "So, why are these people so happy and content?"

"Because in Heaven we feed each other!" replied God.

# Action Steps

1. Look at your goals (personal and professional), and analyze how you can create leverage by involving other people. For example, when I was a stay-at-home mom and wanted to start my own business, I realized that I needed help to achieve it. Initially, I made my parents-in-law and a cleaner part of my "team." As my business and my family grew, so did my team. Because I have a team, I can organize my time in a way that creates a balanced and fulfilling life.

2. Do not be afraid to ask for help or assistance. In life, we should not only be able to give unconditionally but to also accept unconditionally.

3. Finally, remember that the best way to achieve what you want is to help someone else achieve it.

# Using Words with Good Purpose

*Kind words can be short and easy to speak, but their echoes are truly endless.*

—**Mother Teresa**

Did you know that you constantly program yourself and others with the words that you use?

Every word carries energy and emotion with it that positively or negatively affects your life and your environment. Whatever you say, eventually comes back to you like a boomerang; therefore, choosing words carefully when speaking to others and to yourself is another important habit of successful people that I encourage you to adopt.

For example, what is your habitual answer to the common greeting, "How are you?" Do you usually say, "Not too bad," "Fine," "Okay," I'm all right," or do you say, "Fantastic," "Super," "I'm doing great," or "I feel terrific"?

Even if you are not feeling great at that moment, just saying something positive and uplifting makes you and the person who asked feel much better. Positive words also help you manifest experiences that will make you feel positive.

Another example is your habitual way of talking to yourself. Ask yourself, "If a friend spoke to me the way I speak to myself on a regular basis, would I still be his or her friend?"

Finally, be very careful with the words you use when communicating to others! Words often hurt more than punches, and they leave deeper scars. If you don't have something nice to say, don't say anything! Destructive criticism only ensures that the action will be repeated again. Constructive feedback — caring observation with a specific request of the change you want to see – is a lot more effective.

# Action Steps

1. Choose your words carefully. Only speak with good purpose. If it doesn't serve, then don't say it.
2. Encourage others around you to do the same, and surround yourself with positive people.
3. Pay attention to how you speak to yourself. Are you your best friend or your own enemy?
4. Give yourself a ten-day challenge where you speak to yourself *only* in a loving and caring way. You will be surprised how much it will affect your life!

# Personal Satisfaction at Work

*We can change our lives. We can do, have, and be exactly what we wish.*
— **Anthony Robbins**

Do you know what the most frequently mentioned measure of success in work-life is? According to Kouzes and Posner, authors of *The Leadership Challenge*, as surprising as it might sound, it is "personal satisfaction for doing a good job." This reason is cited three to four times as often as "getting ahead" or "making a good living."

Personal satisfaction for doing a good job comes from understanding your purpose and values and aligning them with those of the company you work for. It also comes from being recognized and valued for what you do and who you are.

When we feel that our efforts go unrewarded and unrecognized, it affects our self-esteem and overall performance. At the same time, being dependent on other people for getting recognition can create frustration, dissatisfaction, and even depression.

But, as the Irish author and playwright George Bernard Shaw points out: "People are always blaming their circumstances for what they are. I don't believe in circumstances. The people who get on in this world are the people who get up and look for the circumstances they want, and, if they can't find them, make them."

# Action Steps

1. Clarify your own purpose and values, and make sure your environment supports them.
2. Value yourself and what you do. And remember, the best way to get what you want is to give it first. So, give recognition to people around you, and make them feel valued when opportunity comes.
3. Finally, decide who is in control — you or your circumstances. If you can't find the circumstances that you want, then make them! This is the winning attitude of all successful people.

# Helping Is Not *Always* Good

*A good deed in the wrong place is like an evil deed.*
   —**Marcus Tullius Cicero** (106–43 BC, Roman statesman and writer)

It is important to find a balance in *all* that we do, including helping others. Here is an example of what I mean:

The scoutmaster was listening carefully as the Boy Scouts reported their good deeds for the day.

The first boy stands up and reports that he helped an old lady across the street. "Well done!" says the scoutmaster approvingly.

The next boy stands up and says that he helped the same old lady across the street. Confused, the scoutmaster asks, "Why did it take both of you to help the same lady across the street?"

"That's because she didn't want to go!" replied the boys in unison.

# Action Steps

1. You probably know from your own experience that people will not be receptive to help or advice if they are not ready for it or don't really want it. So, before volunteering your help or advice to someone, ask yourself:

   - What is my intention?
   - Am I really seeing the problem from that person's point of view?
   - Does this person want to be helped?
   - What is the best way to approach this person?
   - When is the best time to do it?

2. What I find works best is first *asking* the person if he or she wants your opinion or advice. Most of the time, people reply yes, and then it is "safe" to proceed, ensuring that your message will come across the way you want it. And if the response is a no, then let it go, and try again another time. As an old saying goes: "Never try to teach a pig to sing. It wastes your time, and it annoys the pig."

# What Is Your Greatness?

*Treat people as if they were what they ought to be, and you help them to become what they are capable of being.*
  —**Johann Wolfgang von Goethe** (1749–1832, German philosopher, poet, and writer)

The importance of valuing your own and other people's differences is demonstrated so well in this parable:

### "The Animal School" by Dr. R. H. Reeves

Once upon a time, the animals decided they must do something heroic to meet the problems of a "New World," so they organized a school. They adopted an activity curriculum consisting of running, climbing, swimming, and flying. To make it easier to administer, all animals took all the subjects.

The duck was excellent in swimming — better, in fact, than his instructor, and he made excellent grades in flying, but he was very poor in running. Since he was low in running, he had to stay after school and also drop swimming to practice running. This was kept up until his webbed feet were badly worn, and he was only average in swimming. But average was acceptable in school, so nobody worried about that except the duck.

The rabbit started at the top of the class in running, but had a nervous breakdown because he had so much to make up in swimming. The squirrel was excellent in climbing until he developed frustrations in the flying class, where his teacher made him start from the ground up instead of from the treetop down. He also developed charley horses from overexertion, and he got a C in climbing and a D in running.

The eagle was a problem child and had to be disciplined severely. In climbing class, he beat all the others to the top of the tree, but he insisted on using his own way of getting there. At the end of the year, an abnormal eel that could swim exceedingly well and could also run, climb, and fly a little had the highest average and was valedictorian.

## Action Steps

1. Do not settle for an average; do not settle for second best. Discover what you are already good at and what you are passionate about and then dedicate all your energy and time to developing your strengths – to achieving your greatness!
2. Be an effective leader, and focus on people's strengths and what they are already good at. Then inspire them to become great at it!

# Are You Busy Being Busy?

*Don't just do something, sit there! Sit there long enough each morning to decide what is really important during the day ahead.*
        —**Sir Richard Eyre** (English film and theatre director)

Do you find yourself busy attending to lots of urgent and important matters but feeling that you are not really going anywhere? Or that you are moving rapidly but not quite sure where? Are you so busy catching up, that life just seems to be passing by without you really having time to reflect on it and enjoy it fully?

Unfortunately, this is the usual scenario of busy executives, parents, business owners, and anyone who is doing his or her best to live up to "life's expectations." Yet, if you wait until you just make a bit more money, or until the children are older, or until business picks up, or until you retire, or until … fill the blank, then *it might never happen!*

When you wait for something to happen in order to do what you want, you voluntarily give up your control over your life and rely, instead, on circumstances. Stop waiting until the "right time," and *make* that time now.

# Action Steps

1. Take out your appointment book, and schedule a daily meeting with your most important client – yourself. Make it an uninterrupted time to just sit and think … just relax and reflect, contemplate, think, feel … just *be*.
2. If you are not used to just *being* because you are always *doing* something, be patient with yourself. It will take time to be able to just sit and do nothing, but it might become the most productive time of your day!

PART 6

JOB

RELIGION

TIME MANAGEMENT & DECISION MAKING

# Effective Decision Making

*To win or lose, to love or hate, to try or quit, to risk or withdraw, to accelerate or hesitate, to dream or stagnate, to open or close, to succeed or fail, to live or die. Every one of these starts with a CHOICE.*

—**Snowden McFall** (author, trainer, and personal coach)

*Regret for the things we did can be tempered by time; it is regret for the things we did not do that is inconsolable.*

—**Sydney J. Harris** (1917–1986, American journalist)

There is nothing in this world that you do in the course of your lifetime that can bring you greater success than the ability to make better choices and decisions. The ability to make choices is one of the most valuable gifts that we, as humans, possess. Since life ultimately consists of making choices, the quality of your life depends on the quality of choices that you make!

If you are not happy with any aspect of your life, then it is up to you to change it. How? By making decisions that carry with them the consequences *you* desire.

Being responsible for your future is an empowering belief! So use your personal power, make sound decisions, and start creating the life you want to have.

# Action Steps

1. The formula for effective decision making is very simple: every decision that moves you *towards* your goals and dreams is an *effective decision*, and every decision that moves you *away* from your goals wastes your valuable time.

2. Next time you find yourself not knowing what decision to make, use this great question for an effective solution: *Does this decision move me closer to the achievement of my goals and my vision or away from them?* The simple process of stopping and asking this question creates a decision-making habit that will help you reach your goals faster. It will eliminate many frustrations and will improve your overall quality of life.

# How Much Do You Rely on Logic?

Do you make decisions using mainly logic, or intuition?

The following parable, called "The Expert," was shared with me by Dr. Bill Gould, the founder of *Transformation Thinking* and a good friend of mine:

> Once there was a group of people who were in the habit of cutting off those heads that contained opinions different from the ones they were pushing at the time. One day they brought along a cart to where they had the guillotine set up. In this cart were three people: a consumer, a businessman, and an "expert."
>
> First, the consumer was put on the guillotine. The lever was pulled, and down came the blade, but it jammed one inch above the consumer's head. The crowd was unanimous: "This was an act of God!" So they let the consumer free, and being a good consumer, he went away muttering about the poor quality of the equipment.
>
> Next, they put the businessman on the guillotine. The lever was pulled, and down came the blade but, once again, it jammed one inch above the businessman's head. Again, the crowd cried out, "Set him free!" and they did. Being a good businessman, he went away with ideas for starting a guillotine repair service.
>
> Finally, they were about to get the "expert," but he leapt up onto the platform and, with a gleam in his eye, he said, "You know, if you would just tighten that screw there and this one here, you will find that the machine will work perfectly" ... and, of course, it did!

Logically, the "expert" was correct, but perhaps there was something inadequate about his *perception* of the situation.

As Dr. Bill Gould points out, logic may often lead us to the correct conclusion, but it is one's overall perception of events that provide the wisdom necessary to arrive at better decisions as to how and when to apply that logic.

## Action Steps

1. Although thinking your decision through logically is good, relying solely on logic can lead to some "painful" experiences. Always listen to your intuition, to your gut, to your sixth sense. Consciously, you might not know all the answers (nor should you strive to have them), but if you are able to connect to the higher power, then you will know the right direction for you to take.

2. Finally, remember that *any* decision is better than indecision.

# Are There Bad Decisions?

Do you believe that there are bad decisions? If yes, what would be a bad decision for you?

My philosophy is that there are no good or bad decisions—there are only consequences. To avoid unwanted consequences, stop and analyze how your decision will affect you in the future.

A decision is like a pebble you toss into a quiet pond. The ripples that emanate from the center and travel outwards in 360 degrees are the effects of that decision. As the ripples flow outwards, they touch everything in their path.

It is the same with your choices and decisions. They affect everyone around you directly or indirectly. What happens when the ripples reach the far shore? They immediately reverse their direction and return to the source. There are many expressions we use to illustrate this concept, such as *What goes around comes around*, or *You reap what you sow*, or *You get back what you put in*.

Once the pebble has left your hand, it is too late to stop the ripples, and they *do* always return to the source. That is why it is so important to consider the consequences and ramifications of what you say and do *before* you commit yourself by your behavior.

And another question to think about — if the ripples that your decision (your pebble) has created touch a leaf on which a frog is sitting, and the frog falls into the water, creating more ripples, who is responsible for those ripples — you or the frog?

The answer is *both*.

# Action Steps

1. Yes, your decisions affect you and those around you, but it is important to not be afraid to make decisions. You see, if you want to "play safe" and not do something because there might be unpleasant consequences, then keep in mind what Dr. Bill Gould said: "There are not only ripples for what we do. There are also ripples for what we should or could have done and didn't."

2. Make brave and effective decisions, take smart risks, and enjoy the journey to your success. In fact, my definition of success *is* this journey!

# The Currency of Today

Effective time management is an integral part to any success. In fact, time is considered the currency of today. Let me share with you a simple but very important tip to getting more done in a shorter time.

Do you find yourself spending a lot of time thinking about what you are not doing and beating yourself up for not doing it? Do you often look forward to doing something particular that you consider fun, recreational, or just more productive, while you are engaged in another activity?

Most of us do. Unfortunately, these kinds of mental activities prevent you from being present with the job at hand, and they waste a lot of your precious time.

The best way to create a clear focus and get your tasks done much more easily and effectively is to follow this rule: Do what you do when you're doing it, and don't do what you're not doing when you're not doing it.

Please read the previous sentence again and let it sink in. Being *in the moment* is not relevant to just the good times; in fact, the more focused you are on the present task at any particular moment, the more productive you are, and the less stress you experience in your life.

# Action Steps

1. If you are eating, take time to enjoy your food.
2. If you are with your children, your spouse, or your friends, just be fully with them; do not worry about what needs to be done and when.
3. If you are working on a project at your job, decide exactly how much you want to achieve in regards to that project, set a deadline, and do not do anything else until you get there.
4. The same applies to everything else, of course.

In our desire to reach our goals and enjoy life when it happens, many of us let life go by. Do not be one of those people.

# Creating a Balanced Life

Are you functioning at your maximum standard of living? Do you want to get more from life? Do you want to give more back?

Many people are so passionate about what they are doing, so focused on their commitment, and so involved in their work, that one part of their lives is a model of excellence, while the rest is in ruin.

Many people understand the value of *balance* and have probably made numerous attempts to achieve it, with good intentions to exercise more, or take a little time off, or to reconnect with friends, but then they find that weeks or months pass without any action.

At today's pace of life, with so many responsibilities, attractive options, demands, and distractions, balance may feel like an impossible dream. Yet, nobody likes to feel "out of balance," and living a balanced life is integral to functioning at your highest standard of living.

# Action Steps

1. If you are working hard to make money and pay the bills, postponing everything else in your life "until the better times," then you are making a big mistake. To create more balance in your life, first realize that getting proper rest, looking after your physical, mental, and emotional well-being, as well as spending quality time with your loved ones, actually adds to your productivity. Once you create this transformational belief, focus on "sharing yourself" equally in all areas of your life.

2. Create weekly schedules. For example, come up with a day of the week and a time that you will dedicate to your most important client – yourself. Do the same for your loved ones, for your career, for your health, and for your goals. Remember, if you do not *make* the time to do something you want to do, then it might never happen.

# The Value of an Hour

*Days are expensive. When you spend a day, you have one less day to spend. So make sure you spend each one wisely.*

—**Jim Rohn**

Do you feel there is not enough time to do what you want to do? For example, you might want to learn a foreign language, get a university degree, exercise more, have more time to be alone and reflect on life, or spend more quality time with your loved ones ...

Before I share with you how to do all those things you lack the time to do, let me ask you this: *How good could you get at something if you did it for the equivalent of just over two months continuously?*

Well, if you invest just one hour each day in your chosen activity, you will accumulate nine forty-hour weeks over the course of just one year (365 days times one hour each is nine 40-hour weeks.)!

In fact, with only an hour a day, over the course of five years, you would have invested the equivalent of 1825 hours of focus on whatever you desire to accomplish in your life! Imagine for a minute, how good you could become at anything that you did one hour a day for the next year!

How fit could you get? How much more love could you get and give? How much more money could you earn?

Is what you want worth investing just one hour a day?

# Action Steps

1. Adopt an hour a day for yourself! If you feel that your schedule is too busy to find that hour, re-evaluate your values and priorities, and remind yourself that you are in control of your life and your time.
2. Pick one area of your life that you want to improve, and commit to focus on it for an hour a day for the next ninety days. I assure you that the results you achieve will be well worth the decision!

And remember ... you can't take out of life more than you put in.

# The Slower You Go, the Faster You Will Get There

Are you so busy focusing on what you want – on the rewards after all that hard work you put in – that you miss out on the journey? Are you going so fast that there is no time to stop and ask yourself *why*?

After landing in the United States as a Soviet refugee in 1987, I went to college and took the entrance test for the ESOL (English for Speakers of Other Languages) program. I was told that my level was minus one. I asked them what that meant, and they said it was below level zero.

In a way, I feel that my journey to success had to start at level minus one because not only did I have nothing to start with (no money, language, contacts, citizenship, or self-esteem), but I had to unlearn all the negative beliefs of the Soviet mentality and propaganda, which made it so much more difficult. Yet, it is my journey that made me who I am today and taught me the lessons that I now share with you. It took me twenty years to get here, but when I think of what I have achieved, the actual time is irrelevant.

If you only focus on the end result, then you do not live your life fully because your mind is always in the future, thinking what needs to be done next. This means that being present in the moment is difficult for you. For example, if you are stuck in traffic, are you usually focused on the destination and on being late, getting stressed and angry, or are you grateful for the opportunity to slow down, look around, and enjoy the moment?

I can imagine you thinking to yourself, "Come on, Masha, why would anyone be grateful for being stuck in traffic?" My answer is, because there is a reason for everything at every step of your journey, and if you are stuck in traffic, maybe it is because you are being protected from an accident ahead of you, or maybe you need that time to reflect on something that might save you hours or years of work.

I used to get upset when I could not sleep at night. Now, I take it as a message to sit and listen, in the silence of the night, to what my subconscious wants to tell me. I usually come up with some great ideas or get an interesting perspective on something that happened that day, which then helps me get to my destination (achieve my goals) much faster and with less stress.

## Action Steps

1. Take the time to stop and reflect on *why* you want what you want. What is the purpose of your journey?

2. When you focus your energies on a worthy purpose and on your journey rather than on the end result, you will get to your destination much faster; you will achieve greater fulfillment, and you will live your life much more fully!

# Are You Living for the Future?

*Life is what happens when we are busy making plans.*
> —**John Lennon** (1940–1980, British singer, songwriter,
> and founder of the Beatles)

Most, if not all, of the great leaders and achievers take plenty of time to relax and reflect. They take time to enjoy life. Do *you*?

So often, we postpone what we really want to do for later. We say to ourselves, "When I have more money ... when I have more time ... when the kids grow up ... when I am not so busy ... when I retire ..." So often, we are living for the future, and yet... the next day is promised to no one!

I knew a man who worked hard and had great plans to travel, to buy a new house, and even to get married after he retired. When he finally retired, he did buy a new house — but he was found dead in it just three weeks later, alone and without a chance to do all those things that he had planned for when the "time was right."

Yes, it is important to think and plan for the future, but it is also just as important to realize that life is happening *now*. So, take time to enjoy life, take time off with your loved ones, take time off for yourself — take time to do *nothing*, to just *be*.

# Action Steps

1. Realize right now that *you* are in control of your life – not your bank statements, not the people around you, not your circumstances. Every decision that you make, and every choice that you have is *yours*.

2. Choose to do something really good for yourself. Take your yearly planner, and schedule in your next vacation. Whether you think you can do it or not, just schedule it in, make plans for it, and see how it will work out for you.

3. Make an appointment with yourself. Decide on an hour each day that is just for you to do what feeds your soul. If you can take more time, great. If you can't find an hour, start with twenty minutes, and then add to it.

Remember, it's the space *between* the notes that makes the music.

PART 7

THE BEST SOURCE OF WEALTH

# Produce the Results You Are Looking For

*The definition of insanity is doing the same thing over and over again and expecting different results.*
—**Albert Einstein** (1879–1955, one of the greatest physicists of all time)

Did you know that, statistically, over 90% of people give up on their goals and New Year resolutions within three weeks of setting them? Did you ever wonder *why* so many people who set goals and New Year resolutions, one year later realize that what they set for themselves they haven't accomplished?

Then, with new enthusiasm, they do it again, just to get disappointed later. It becomes a vicious circle, and, unfortunately, many people eventually give up making goals in life. They would rather not have goals than feel bad for not following through with them.

Unfortunately, when this happens, people tend to think that something is wrong with *them*! Their self-esteem goes down, and low self-esteem is one of the major reasons for not succeeding. But here is some good news: not following through with goals has *nothing* to do with who you are.

If you have a great desire to succeed but are not getting what you want, then you are simply lacking the right tools. By tools, I mean the necessary knowledge, skills, and mindset – all of which, fortunately, you can acquire!

When you stop blaming yourself for not having what you want and start learning all you can in the area that you want to change, you will inevitably become the kind of person who attracts what you desire and produces the results you are looking for!

# Action Steps

1. Help yourself grow and develop in the direction you want to go. Decide how much time and money you will dedicate this year to personal development.
2. Decide what it is you really want to learn, and then find appropriate courses and/or teachers for it.
3. Do it today! If you expect different results, then do things differently, be proactive, and be persistent!

# What Did You Miss Out On Today?

*If a man empties his purse into his head, no man can take it away from him. An investment in knowledge always pays the best interest.*

**—Benjamin Franklin** (1706–1790, one of the best known Founding Fathers of the United States)

*We've all heard the phrase "creature of habit." That can be good or bad, depending on your habits. I've cultivated the learning habit over the years, and it's one of the most pleasurable aspects of my life.*

**—Donald Trump**

One of the things that successful people have in common is their passion for learning. When Donald Trump, who was named the Hotel and Real Estate Visionary of the Century by the UJA Federation, was asked what keeps him going, he replied, "If I end the day without knowing more than I did when I woke up, it makes me wonder: What did I miss out on today? Am I getting lazy? I am a disciplined person, and this thought alone can get me going."

In his book *Trump: How to Get Rich*, Mr. Trump points out that "Every day is a reminder to me of how much I don't know. Everything I learn leads me to something else I didn't know. Fortunately, I don't pride myself on being a know-it-all, so every day becomes a new challenge."

Henry Ford said, "If money is your hope for independence, you will never have it. The only real security that a man will have in this world is a reserve of knowledge, experience, and ability."

Clint Eastwood once remarked: "I'd like to be a bigger and more knowledgeable person ten years from now than I am today. I think that, for all of us, as we grow older, we must discipline ourselves to continue expanding, broadening, learning, keeping our minds active and open."

# Action Steps

1. Make time for reading about topics that interest and inspire you. As Jim Rohn points out: "The only thing worse than not reading a book in the last ninety days is not reading a book in the last ninety days and thinking that it doesn't matter."
2. At least twice a year, attend a workshop or a seminar. Not only will you pick up new ideas and increase your knowledge base, but also you will meet like-minded people and often make long-lasting friendships.
3. Cultivate the learning habit, and inspire others to do the same. Before you go to bed, ask yourself, "What did I learn today?" Write the answer down in your journal, and review it regularly. It is very empowering!

# The Power of Questions

*The quality of our lives is closely related to the quality of our questions.*
—**Michael Angier** (speaker and founder of Success Networks)

- What is wrong with me?
- Why does this always happen to me?
- Why don't I like myself?
- I am such an idiot! Why did I have to do that?

Do you find yourself asking these kinds of questions in your day-to-day life? Many people do. It seems easier, or even more honorable in some way, to beat yourself up rather than praise yourself for a job well done. Why?

Although it might be interesting for you to analyze why that is happening, it is more important to understand that, whatever you ask your brain, it *will* find you an answer! It is just the way your brain operates. Understanding that, you can use it to your advantage rather than disadvantage.

If you ask your brain *What is wrong with me?* then your brain will reply with a lot of very good answers, even if they are not real — just because you asked!

What if, instead, you asked yourself questions such as these:

- What is good about me?
- What did I do to deserve all these wonderful things in my life?
- What can I do or think to like myself more?
- I am only human, and I made a mistake. How can I learn from it?

Whatever you ask, you will get an answer. Whatever you focus on becomes your reality. Use the power of questions to get the answers you *really* want!

# Action Steps

1. Come up with five empowering and motivational questions to prepare yourself each morning for the successful day ahead of you.
2. Change your questions every ten days, depending on what answers you want to know at a particular time in your life. Some sample questions are as follows:
   - Who or what in my life makes me feel the happiest?
   - How can I make enough money within six months to buy the car that I want?
   - How can I be a better leader today?
   - What can I do today to make my loved ones happy?

# Ask and You Will Receive

*Quality questions create a quality life. Successful people ask better questions and as a result, they get better answers.*

**—Anthony Robbins**

Continuing on the topic of questions, let me give you an example of how you can use questions to attract more success in your personal life and your business.

One of my clients, Justin, wanted to increase his sales and produce better results at work. At the time, he was selling insurance and was getting three to five new clients a month.

Following my advice, he came up with a specific question, "How can I increase my client-base by fifty clients within nine months?" He then wrote twenty-one answers to that question. By writing as many as twenty-one answers to that question, he gained a competitive advantage over others by coming out with some creative ideas that most people would not take the time to think about.

In the first month, he got nine new clients, and in six and a half months, he reached his target of fifty clients. He was appointed a team leader and taught his team the same simple principle of asking specific questions and writing down twenty-one answers. Soon, Justin's team became the best sales team in the company.

Within a year, Justin had more than doubled his paycheck and had received a company bonus. He kept asking questions such as "How can I attract more quality clients?" "How can I resolve this problem in the best way possible?" "What can I do to retire in ten years with five million dollars in assets and residual income?"

As Justin said himself, "I never worry anymore where my next client will come from and how I'll find the money to invest in the next project. I just know that if I keep my focus on the question, the answer always comes."

You, too, can undertake and successfully accomplish any project or endeavor, resolve any problem, and reach your goals much faster by learning how to use the power of questions and having faith that the answer will always come.

## Action Steps

1. How can *you* use the power of questions to produce desired results in *your* life?
2. Simply make quality questions one of your empowering habits and, as a result, enjoy a better quality of life!

# Excellence Is Not an Act, But a Habit

*We are what we repeatedly do. Excellence then, is not an act, but a habit.*
—**Aristotle** (384–322 BC, Greek philosopher)

Most people do not realize what kind of power our habits hold over us! That is because what you do habitually is often unconscious; yet, your habits constantly express your character and the results you produce (or do not produce) on a regular basis.

Most of what people do in life is habitual. Since your current habits can only get you what you are already getting, for you to reach your goals, however small or big they are, it is necessary to create new habits or to eliminate the ones that do not serve you.

Basically, if you want to change your life, then you need to change your habits!

Stephen R. Covey, the author of the well-known best seller, *The Seven Habits of Highly Effective People*, defines a habit as the intersection of knowledge, skill, and desire. He describes his terms as follows:

- *Knowledge* is the "what to do" and the "why."
- *Skill* is the "how to do."
- *Desire* and motivation are the "want to do."

In order to make something a habit in your life, all three ingredients must be present.

No matter what you want in your life, chances are that someone out there already has it. Find these people. Study and understand their habits and their belief systems. In essence, to become a millionaire, study and adopt the millionaire's money habits; to be fit and healthy, study and adopt the habits of those who are fit and healthy.

# Action Steps

1. The first step is to decide which habit you would like to change or adopt and why it is essential for you to do it. For example, you might want to adopt the habit of exercising twenty minutes a day, because it will help you lose weight, increase your energy, and shape your body, which, in turn, will make you feel good about yourself, increase your self-esteem, and make you more successful in all areas of your life.

2. Now you will need to develop the skill that will allow you to achieve that goal and build a new habit — you will need to learn "how to do it." In the above example, you could learn from a personal trainer or a DVD, or you could even partner up with someone who already has the habit and can pass it on to you, which is always an excellent idea!

3. The final ingredient is the desire. You have to be motivated enough to consciously push yourself to do what you've learned, in order to build this new habit for at least thirty days (forty recommended). This is usually how long it takes for your brain to adopt a new habit. It is very important that you practice the new habit for thirty *consecutive* days, or you have to start all over again.

Is it worth the trouble? Well, that all depends on how badly you want to live the life of your dreams — if you chose to settle for "good enough" or go for "extraordinary" instead. As always, the choice is *yours*!

# You Have the Power – Mind Power!

*Formal education will make you a living; self-education will make you a fortune.*

—Jim Rohn

*The future belongs to those who have learned how to learn.*

—Masha Malka

What is the best source of wealth? Is it gold, land, factories, or real estate? Actually, the best source of wealth is not contained in material possessions but in between your ears – it is your *mind power*, as well as your ability to learn and acquire knowledge better and faster than others.

If you do not update your skills and knowledge on an ongoing basis, then you put yourself in a position of living in fear of uncertainty, afraid of getting fired or blaming circumstances for whatever is happening in your life.

I find it very interesting that my clients tend to be men and women who are already successful. Maybe they are successful because they understand that the only way to move forward, the only way to overcome current obstacles, and the only way to improve their quality of life is by acquiring new knowledge and skills.

Also, people who have reached a certain goal once (like becoming a millionaire), find it much easier to do it the second time because they have learned the formula.

What will *you* learn today to make your life better tomorrow?

# Action Steps

1. Although knowledge is powerful, it is not much use unless you *act* on it! In your journal, write down at the top of the page: "How can I increase my knowledge in my chosen topic?" It can relate to your work, or it can also be about relationships, self-discovery, success, or anything else that you are currently thinking about and would like to know more about.

2. After you have written that question, write twenty-one answers/action steps below. Choose five action steps from that list, and act on them within a week. Then, continue with the rest of the steps.

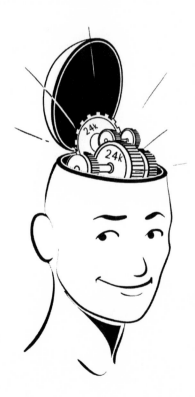

PART 8

IT IS NEVER TOO LATE

# You Make a Difference!

*Sharing makes you bigger than you are. The more you pour out, the more life will be able to pour in.*

—Jim Rohn

Did you ever think about making a difference in this world but felt you were not powerful enough to do that? Let me tell you a story that might change your mind, about sharing and making a difference:

As a man was walking along a sandy beach, completely engrossed in his thoughts, he suddenly found himself amongst thousands of starfish that were washed up on shore. He thought to himself for a moment, *how cruel nature can be*, but he felt powerless to the fact that all those starfish would be dead before the day was gone.

He continued walking and reflecting on his life, thinking back to all the times he had tried to make a difference but had never managed to come out on top.

Still deep in his thoughts, he noticed a woman in the distance picking up starfish and throwing them back into the ocean, one by one. He decided to walk up to her and ask her what she was doing. The woman replied that she enjoyed making a difference, and this was a perfect opportunity to do so.

"There are thousands of starfish on the beach, and many more are being washed up every minute," replied the man. "How can you possibly be making a difference?"

The woman silently bent down, picked up another starfish, and threw it back into the ocean. "I made a difference to *that* one!" she finally replied, smiling kindly.

# Action Steps

1. To make a difference, one does not have to wait for some big moment, for when the time is right, or for when there is more money to donate or more time to give. You have the opportunities and the power to make a difference every day of your life. Compliment someone, smile, give your undivided attention when someone speaks to you, let people know how much they mean to you, and share this book with them. The list of small things that can make a big difference is endless …

2. Commit right now to add to someone's happiness today and every day *unconditionally*, and don't forget to include *yourself* on that list!

# Can One Person Change the World?

*You are where you are and what you are because of what you believe yourself to be. Change your beliefs and you change your reality.*

—**Brian Tracy**

Continuing on the topic of making a difference, do *you* believe one person can change the world? Do you believe it can be you?

In 1988, I was just a little Russian girl in the big and powerful country of the United States of America. I felt insignificant and not very powerful. Although I always wanted to make a difference and change the world, I wondered what I could possibly do without even speaking the language! Then, while in college, I came across this interesting research, and it changed my perspective. Let me share it with you.

In 1961, Edward Lorenz, a research meteorologist at the Massachusetts Institute of Technology, conducted an experiment. He was using a numerical computer model to rerun a weather prediction. Feeling tired, he took a shortcut on a number in the sequence, and instead of entering the full number .506127, he entered the decimal .506, assuming that this tiny difference (one part in a thousand) would not make a significant difference to his report. However, this slight change produced an overwhelmingly different output!

The result was such a different weather scenario that, in his New York Academy of Sciences article in 1963, Mr. Lorenz concluded that "If the theory were correct, one flap of a seagull's wings could change the course of weather forever." In later speeches and papers, Edward Lorenz replaced the seagull with a butterfly, thus naming his theory "The Butterfly Effect." In a 1972 academic paper, he describes how the flap of a butterfly's wings in Brazil can set off a tornado in Texas!

Why did this research affect me so much? Because what it basically means is that if a butterfly can be so powerful in changing the weather patterns and therefore the world, how powerful can I be? How much change can I and each of us create just by one action? One thought? One intention? What if we did it consistently?

Since then, one of my purposes in life has become "to change the world for the better by becoming the best I can be; by changing myself for the better, I inevitably change the world!"

## Action Step

Understand that everything you do and even think affects this world. *How* you will affect it, is up to you!

# NOW is The Right Time

*It is never too late to be what you might have been.*

—**George Eliot** (1819–1880, English novelist)

Have you ever felt like it was too late to follow your dreams? Too late to discover and live the life of your purpose? If you have, then this story might inspire you:

> Good morning, professor," said the young student, as the older man entered the classroom. Taken by surprise, the older man sat beside his fellow students and said, "I am not a professor; I am a medical student just like you, and today is my first day!"
>
> One of the students quickly responded, "Medical student? May I ask how old you are?"
>
> "I am seventy-three," replied the older man, with a twinkle in his eye. "I always wanted to be a doctor, and I'm finally ready to follow my dream!"
>
> "With all due respect," continued the student, "by the time you graduate, you will be eighty years old!"
>
> The older man put his hand on the young man's shoulder and said, "God willing, I will be eighty years old whether I go after my dreams or not!"

I always say to myself and to others that it is better to be truly happy and fulfilled for one hour than never. It is better to strive and work hard towards an inspiring goal than always wonder "what if …?"

I know people who started to follow their dreams after they retired, and they became super successful in every way. I know people who fell madly in love at almost seventy years old, got married, and now live blissfully happy lives …

It is *never* too late. The only limitations you have are the limitations of your own mind and your belief system!

## Action Step

Have the courage to go after your heart's desires and experience what real fulfillment and happiness are.

# CONCLUSION

## The Most Important Job You Do

*Make the most of yourself, for that is all there is of you.*
**—Ralph Waldo Emerson** (1803–1882, American author, poet, and philosopher)

What is the most important job that you do? I believe that the most important job you do is the one that is unheard and unseen! The most important job you do happens *within*.

It is the journey to becoming the best you can be. It is becoming the kind of person who attracts all that you want in life. The most important job you do, is getting to know yourself — who *you* are and what *you* want to have, to do, and to *be* in this life.

You become the best you can be by taking your time to be with yourself, to understand your wants and needs, and to understand and honor your uniqueness.

You do it by realizing that *you* are in control of your life and your future and by taking consistent actions to create that future — taking full responsibility rather than blaming circumstances.

# Action Steps

1. Before you move on to the next page, before you close this book and immerse yourself into your day-to-day tasks, please take your calendar and schedule a date ... with *yourself*! It doesn't matter if you schedule a full day or just twenty minutes. As long as you know that this time is just for *you* — to do what you want, to think what you want, and to just be. It is the time to honor yourself as someone important enough to be with.

2. Make an ongoing date, a time or a day you can look forward to. Be patient, be good to yourself, and enjoy the journey!

**The One Minute Coach**™

# SPECIAL BONUS OFFER

To THANK YOU for purchasing my book and for your dedication to your growth, I would like to offer you the following:

1. **"Good Intentions Do Not Last"** Web Seminar
2. Subscription to **The One Minute Coach** e-program
3. An opportunity to win an intensive ONE-ON-ONE **"Six Weeks to Freedom"** coaching program

Total value $1,267; **YOURS absolutely FREE!**

To receive your BONUSES please go to
**www.mashamalka.com/bookbonuses**

In the **"Good Intentions Do Not Last"** Web Seminar, discover the reasons most people give up on their goals and New Year resolutions and what to do about that.

**The One Minute Coach** weekly e-program is designed to keep your motivation going, through inspirational and educational messages followed by action steps, just as it is done in this book.

The ONE-ON-ONE **"Six Weeks to Freedom"** coaching program **with Masha Malka** helps you achieve the most important freedom of all—the freedom within—the freedom to be who you are!

Find out more at www.mashamalka.com/bookbonuses

Looking forward to hearing from you!

Your partner in success,
Masha Malka

# THANK YOU!

I am very grateful to everyone who helped me make one of my big dreams come true – to create and publish this book. I would like to personally thank and acknowledge these amazing people here; without them, this book would still be a dream …

- Doron Malka, my husband and my best friend, for loving me unconditionally, for supporting me in every way, and for all the help with the book's editing, design, and printing.
- Vladimir Yarosh, my father, for financing the book and believing in me, for his love and support, and for never saying "no" to me.
- Larissa Abrams, my mother, for her unconditional love and support, which bring me security and peace, helping me overcome many fears and doubts.
- Rick Yarosh, my brother, as well as my wonderful friend and ally, for his high expectations of me that always encourage me to strive for more, and for being my inspiration in many ways.
- Veronica, Julia, and David, my children, for bringing so much joy into my life and making it all worthwhile …
- Anna Polonsky, the book's artist and designer, for being such a genius and understanding what I need, often without my even saying it!
- Cary Johnston, the book's editor, for believing in me and for caring so much about this book and giving it his personal touch.
- Renée Coppinger, my personal stylist and my best friend, for her talent and expertise as a stylist, for always being there for me, and for supporting me unconditionally.
- Rick Frishman, one of the leading book publicists in America, for "discovering me" and introducing *The One Minute Coach* to Morgan James Publishing, and for his easygoing and ingenious advice and support.

- David Hancock, founder of Morgan James Publishing, for making me a part of his publishing family, for caring so much about this book's destiny, and for playing a big part in it!
- Morgan James Publishing team, for all their help, work, and assistance.
- My wonderful friends from different parts of the world, who probably believe in me more than I believe in myself and who constantly encouraged me with such statements as these: "So when is the book going to be ready? I am sure it will be a best seller! I can't wait to read it!" A big thank-you to Sheri Haman, Cindy Barnes, Louise Cook, Marianne de Witt, Mary Harboe, Barbara Page Roberts, Chani Goldstein, and Veronica Butsina.
- My teachers who have inspired me and shaped me in many ways — they are the people I admire and look up to: Anthony Robbins, Brian Tracy. Oprah Winfrey, Mark Victor Hansen, Bill Clinton, Donald Trump, Barbara de Angelis, Jack Canfield, Hale Dwoskin, Dr. Bill Gould, and Adi Gunawan.
- Gary Edwards, renowned photographer, for taking beautiful photos of me and my family and for his generosity.
- Robert Schwartz, patent attorney and father of two wonderful girls — Elise and Gerry (whom I used to babysit and teach), for always making himself available when I needed his legal advice and expertise.
- Miranda Rijnsburger, a wonderful mother of five and my friend, for being a true inspiration on how to combine motherhood and career.
- Michael Izotov, our family doctor, for looking after my family so well!
- Cheryl Alexander Sterns, my life coach, for very timely, positive infusions and for her wisdom and advice.
- Subscribers of *The One Minute Coach* newsletter, for giving me the confidence to go on sharing my beliefs and my passion and for compiling my messages into this book.
- Finally, *you* the reader, for the trust you put in me and for helping me to fulfill my purpose. Thank you!

# RECOMMENDED READING

These are some of the books and programs that have influenced and changed my life. Many of the books and authors below are also mentioned and quoted throughout *The One Minute Coach*.

**The 7 Habits of Highly Effective People,** by Stephen Covey

**The 11th Element: The Key to Unlocking Your Master Blueprint for Wealth and Success,** by Robert Scheinfeld

**The 100 Absolutely Unbreakable Laws of Business Success,** by Brian Tracy

**Abundance for Life: Trance Breaking, Wealth Making,** by Paul R. Scheele

**Accelerated Learning** (audio program), by Colin Rose and Brian Tracy

**The Alchemist,** by Paulo Coelho

**Awaken the Giant Within,** by Anthony Robbins

**The Celestine Prophecy,** by James Redfield

**Change Your Life in 7 Days,** by Paul McKenna

**Chicken Soup for the Soul,** by M. Victor Hansen and Jack Canfield

**Conversations with God,** by Neale Donald Walsch

**The Einstein Factor** by Win Wenger and Richard Poe

**The Empty Chair: Finding Hope and Joy,** by Rabbi Nachman of Breslov

**Focal Point,** by Brian Tracy

**The Greatest Salesman in the World,** by Og Mandino

**How to Get Rich,** by Donald J. Trump

**How to Win Friends and Influence People,** by Dale Carnegie

**The Leadership Challenge,** by J. M. Kouzes and B. Z Posner

**Leadership Wisdom from the Monk Who Sold His Ferrari,** by Robin Sharma

**Life 101: Everything We Wish We Had Learned about Life in School But Didn't,** by Peter McWilliams

**The Little Book of Coaching: Motivating People to Be Winners,** by Ken Blanchard and Don Shula

**Many Lives, Many Masters,** by Brian L. Weiss

**Master Thinker Program** (workshop), by Dr. Bill Gould

**The One Minute Manager,** by Kenneth H. Blanchard and
  Spencer Johnson

**The One Minute Millionaire** by Victor Hansen and Robert G. Allen

**Personal Power II: The Driving Force** (audio program),
  by Anthony Robbins

**The Power of Purpose,** by Richard Leider

**The Prophet,** by Kahlil Gibran

**The Psychology of Achievement** (audio program), by Brian Tracy

**A Return to Love: Reflections on the Principles of "A Course
  in Miracles,"** by Marianne Williamson

**Rich Dad, Poor Dad,** by Robert Kiyosaki

**The Seat of the Soul,** by Gary Zukav

**Secrets about Men Every Woman Should Know,** by Barbara de Angelis

**The Sedona Method: Your Key to Lasting Happiness, Success, Peace,
  and Emotional Well-Being,** by Hale Dwoskin

**Think and Grow Rich,** by Napoleon Hill

**Who Moved My Cheese?** by Spencer Johnson and
  Kenneth H. Blanchard

Please visit http://www.mashamalka.com/recommendations.php to read
a summary for each of these books and/or to purchase them.

Thank you!

# ABOUT THE AUTHOR

Masha Malka is an entrepreneur, a success coach, speaker, and founder and writer of *The One Minute Coach* e-program, author of the e-book *Discover Your Inborn Genius, as well as a mother of three children.*

Living and working in the diverse cultures of **six countries** (Russia, United States, Austria, England, Bulgaria, and Spain) has given her a unique insight on **how to achieve success,** regardless of cultural background.

Masha deeply believes that **we** are all potential geniuses and that we are capable of achieving **success** in *all* areas of our lives, leading to greater **happiness, fulfillment,** and **peace of mind.**

She dedicates her life to helping people create balance and positivity on the way to their dream lives. She also encourages and helps people to unleash their potential and achieve their greatness.

**Please visit www.mashamalka.com to find out more.**

# ABOUT THE ARTIST

Anna Polonsky is a young artist who graduated from the Art Institute of Fort Lauderdale, Florida, in 2008. She specializes in the latest computer software of both 2D and 3D art and also has great passion for the traditional arts of painting, illustration, and sculpture. Anna is continuously engaged in creating new works of art, exhibiting them alongside acknowledged contemporary artists and is on her way to becoming recognized with her own distinguished style. With roots in both Russia and Israel, where Anna has relatives and friends, she is an open and multicultural person.

Anna is driven by the vision of creating works of art that will motivate people and artists alike to open their minds towards the realm of imagination and the power of thought.

Working with Masha on this incredibly empowering book has truly had a positive impact on Anna's lifestyle and art, inspiring her to make every image in this book into something that will inspire others.

To contact Anna, please write to: evilanka@gmail.com
or visit www.polonskyart.com

Printed in the United States
129445LV00002B/1/P